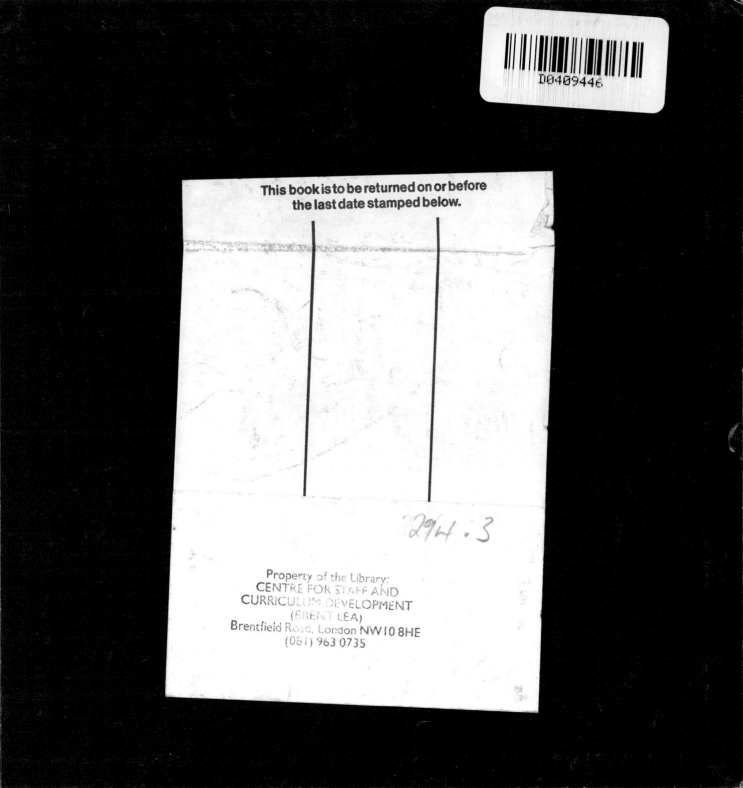

This book is to be returned on or before
the last date stamped below.

Smith, Linda
Dat's New Year.—(Celebrations)
1. New Year—China—Juvenile literature
2. New Year—Great Britain—Juvenile literature
I. Title   II. Series
394.2'683   GT4905

ISBN 0–7136–2644–5

Published by A & C Black (Publishers) Ltd
35 Bedford Row, London WC1R 4JH

Acknowledgements
The author and publishers would like to thank Mr Dang Phuoc Tri, and the
Society for Anglo-Chinese Understanding for their help and advice, the staff and
pupils of Parsloes Primary and, most of all, Dat and the Tran family.

ISBN 0-7136-2644-5

Filmset by August Filmsetting, Haydock, St Helens
Printed in Hong Kong by Dai Nippon Printing Co. Ltd

Dat's New Year

Linda Smith

Photographs by Sally Fear

A & C Black · London

My name is Dat.
I'm five years old,
but I'll soon be six.

Here I am with my big
brothers, Huy and Vy.
We're helping Mum and
Dad to put up decorations
for New Year.

Dad's the tallest so he
puts up the paper-chains.

I'm putting up the lanterns
with a bit of help from Huy.

3

It takes a long time to put up all the decorations.
Huy is in a hurry because he wants to go to
football practice.

Mum says she's tired of decorating and she
needs a rest.

Dad has bought some flowers for her.
It's supposed to be lucky if a flower opens up
on New Year's Day.

Our New Year is the first day on the Chinese
calendar. Only two more days to go!

Dad helps me to write some New Year cards.
We write one to Uncle Tu in London and one to
Grandad. He lives in Vietnam.

Dad writes the envelopes, but I write on the cards.

This one says 'Sun Nee Fie Lo'. That's Chinese for
'Happy New Year!'

The next day, I take my card
to school.

Lee and Jane think it's a good idea
to make their own cards.
Then everyone wants to try!

Vy helps us to write on our cards. He can read and write Chinese.

Huy and Vy both learn Chinese at Sunday school in London. I can't go because I'm always sick on the train, so Dad teaches me at home.

We are writing 'Fu' on our cards.
It means 'blessing' and it looks like this. 福

We're making some New Year decorations, too. Baldesh shows us how to make the flowers. Her mum told her how to do it.

Then we try to make some wall hangings like the ones at home. They don't look quite right but our teacher, Mrs Joynes, likes them.

Mrs Joynes tells our class about the Chinese calendar.
Each year is named after an animal.
There are twelve animals altogether.
This year it's the rat's turn.

Look at us!
We've made a mask for each animal.

Kaimba's rat mask makes everyone laugh. The rat's eyes are lop-sided and one ear is too big. But Mrs Joynes doesn't think it's very funny.

We paint a big circle with one part for each animal. Everyone looks to see which year they were born in. I was born in the year of the horse.

Tonight is New Year's Eve and Mum is cooking a big dinner.

I've asked Robert to come round. He's my best friend at school.

My brothers' friends come too. When we all sit down, it's a bit of a squash.

Mum says that New Year was different when
we lived in Vietnam. We lived with
Grandmother and Grandfather and on New
Year's Day the whole family came round.

I don't remember Vietnam though. We came
to England when I was a tiny baby.

After dinner we have just enough room left for
sweets and oranges.

I'm in a hurry to finish. I want to open my lucky
money envelope. Uncle Tu always sends me one
at New Year.

Mum has put my envelope on top of a cake. When I open it, there is five pounds inside. Enough for a new football!

Robert's mum lets him stay late so we play games and try to stay up until midnight.

The best part of New Year is our trip to London. Mum and Dad take us to see the big New Year parade.

When we get there, it's very crowded. I can see people standing on the roofs.

We stay close to Mum and Dad in case we get lost.

We have to wait around for a long time. I keep asking Dad when the dragon will arrive. But he just says 'Wait and see'. He always says that.

Mum buys us some toffee-apples while we're waiting.

I climb up on Dad's
shoulders. It's safer
there and I can see
much better.

Dad isn't looking very
hard so I'm the first
one to see the dragon.

It isn't a real dragon, of
course. There are men
inside it. But they
make the dragon
move and turn as if it
was alive.

18

After the dragon there is a big furry lion. They stop at all the shops to collect long strings of money.
Dad says it's lucky if the dragon stops outside your house.

Robert wants to give some money to the lion, but Mum says that we shouldn't go too close.

On Monday we have our school New Year party. Mum comes to school with me. She cooks us chicken, rice and peas for dinner.

It's much better than school dinners. Even Mrs Joynes says so.

Mum shows everyone how to eat with chopsticks. It's easy when you know how. Baldesh is very good at it.

But Lee gets his fingers and his chopsticks all mixed up. Kaimba wants a spoon instead. He says that using chopsticks is too slow.

We're going to make a dragon to show to
all our mums and dads.

David and Di make the head from
cardboard and egg boxes.

Then we paint the dragon green.
It's very messy, but the dragon looks great.

I'm feeding the dragon with paper money, just like
they did in London.

Robert says that next New Year we could make a
lion, too. Then we could visit people's houses.
But Mrs Joynes says we'll have to wait and see.

Things to do

There are lots of things in this book which you could try for yourself, like making Chinese New Year cards, or decorations. Here are some more things which you may like to try.

1. Many people all over the world celebrate New Year at different times. Try to find out about some different New Year celebrations. How do you celebrate New Year and why do you think it is important? Compare stories with your friends.

2. An old Chinese legend tells how each year came to be named after an animal. Ask someone to tell you the story (see books below) and find out which animal rules the year when you were born.

Depending on which animal rules the year when you were born, you are supposed to be a certain kind of person. What does this remind you of? Try to find out about the signs of the Zodiac.

Do you think that you can tell what someone is like from the month or year when they were born?

3. Find out more about Chinese food and how it is cooked. You could try to make some for yourself.

Do you have special food at New Year? What about your friends? You could make a New Year recipe book.

4. Some people think that dragons are frightening creatures. But in Chinese legend, the dragon is a king and a symbol of good luck. You can read about the Chinese dragon in some of the stories at the bottom of this page. Try making your own dragon or Chinese lion.

Glossary

Chinese New Year (or Spring Festival) is celebrated by Chinese communities all over the world.

In traditional households, a week before New Year the Kitchen God is believed to ascend to heaven to make his yearly report on the family's behaviour. While he is away, the house is cleaned and new clothes are bought; debts are paid and disagreements settled. On New Year's Eve, the Kitchen God returns and the evening is celebrated with a special meal.

The Chinese Calendar. The date of Chinese New Year changes each year because it is based on the first day of the lunar calendar. In China, this calendar is still used for festivities and birthdays.

Chinese language. There are several different Chinese languages, for example, Cantonese, Fukien and Mandarin. Although these languages sound very different from one another, they are all written down in the same way. Written Chinese uses characters and each character represents an idea rather than the sound of a word.

Books to read

A Book of Dragons, *by R.L. Green* (Penguin)
Stop that Dragon, *by M. Hynds* (Blackie)
Chun's Chinese Dragon, *by J. Holiday* (Hamish Hamilton)
Phoenix Bird Chinese Take-away, *by K. Mackinnon* (A & C Black)
Stories from Ancient China, *by Heaton/West* (Longman)
Chinese New Year, (Barking and Dagenham Language Unit, Station Parade, Barking Essex)
The Chinese New Year Story (Minority Group Support Unit, South Street, Hillfields, Coventry)